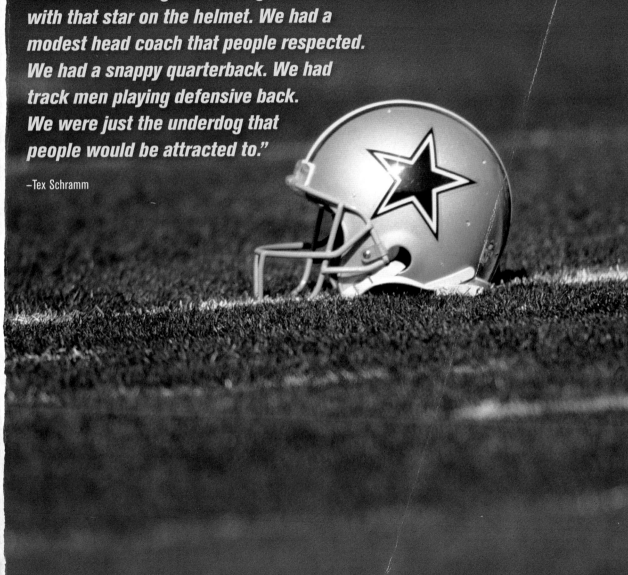

"We captured people's imagination
because we had good-looking uniforms
with that star on the helmet. We had a
modest head coach that people respected.
We had a snappy quarterback. We had
track men playing defensive back.
We were just the underdog that
people would be attracted to."

–Tex Schramm

Stewart, Tabori & Chang
New York

101 REASONS TO LOVE THE
COWBOYS

RON GREEN, JR.

INTRODUCTION

Like Coca-Cola and the Empire State Building, the Dallas Cowboys are more than American—they *are* America. Like cheeseburgers and state fairs, Friday night lights and Thanksgiving Day parades, the Cowboys represent a city, a state, and a country that love their football, especially if the helmets are silver with a navy blue star on each side.

The Cowboys long ago became "America's Team" because of both their style and their success. The Cowboys have always had a swagger, a confidence that fits the people from whom the franchise is nicknamed. They're not from New York City or Los Angeles, where stars gather. They're from deep in the heart of Texas, where football lives.

The Cowboys are more than a franchise. They are a brand, every bit as identifiable as Apple or General Motors. It doesn't mean everyone loves the Cowboys. Perhaps no NFL team inspires as much loathing as the Cowboys, a testament to who they are and how they play. Although they've won five Super Bowls and helped define the golden era of professional football, the Cowboys' popularity transcends their win-loss record.

In what amounted to the dark ages of the franchise, shortly after Jerry Jones bought the team and jettisoned the creators, including Tom Landry, Tex Schramm, and Gil Brandt, the Cowboys went 1–13. To Washington Redskins fans and some others, it was a beautiful time. But something was missing from the NFL—the Cowboys.

They don't have to win every game or every championship, but they need to be relevant— and, of course, they were again. The Cowboys aren't always ideal, but they represent an ideal. They are big, shiny, and strong. They're Tom Landry's fedora, Roger Staubach's self-confidence, and Bullet Bob Hayes. They're Randy White, Lee Roy Jordan, and Bob Lilly. They're Troy Aikman, Emmitt Smith, and Michael Irvin.

The Cowboys are a brand as big as owner Jerry Jones' dreams and as small as the star-emblazoned onesies that babies wear in places like Lubbock, Luckenbach, and Little Rock. They're the Cowboys.

Here are 101 reasons to love them. It's just a start.

Members of the U.S. Navy hold up an American flag before a game between the San Diego Chargers and the Dallas Cowboys, 2010.

1 AMERICA'S TEAM

On the surface, it's a presumptuous nickname, but it's come to be a part of the Cowboys' legacy. The team didn't brand itself in the Stars and Stripes. It was the result of an introduction to an NFL Films highlight piece in 1978. Bob Ryan, an executive with NFL Films, is credited with giving the Cowboys their nickname.

The intro went like this: "They appear on television so often that their faces are as familiar to the public as presidents and movie stars. They are the Dallas Cowboys, America's Team." Others have tried through the years to claim the distinction—or they've had it put on them—but it hasn't stuck. It belongs to the Dallas Cowboys.

2 THE STAR

It's the symbol of the Dallas Cowboys, a blue star on each side of their iconic helmets that stands for more than just a football team. It's a tribute to Texas, the Lone Star State, and to the franchise that is one of the most popular sports teams in the world. It's instantly recognizable and helps define a franchise that has been as rich in star power as it has in popularity and success.

3 BIRTH OF THE COWBOYS

The Cowboys were born at a meeting of NFL owners in Miami Beach in 1960, the same meeting that produced a compromise candidate named Pete Rozelle as the league's new commissioner and granted Minnesota a franchise to begin play in 1961. The Dallas franchise was owned by Clint Murchison Jr. and Bedford Wynne, and Tex Schramm was chosen to be general manager. Tom Landry, a defensive coordinator with the New York Giants, was hired as head coach once the franchise became a reality. Not everyone in Dallas was overjoyed by the Cowboys' creation. The new American Football League had just established a team in Dallas— the Dallas Texans—and when the NFL announced it was coming to town, AFL commissioner Joe Foss called it "an act of war." Three years later, the Texans surrendered Dallas to the Cowboys and moved to Kansas City, where they changed their nickname to the Chiefs.

4 THE ORIGINAL OWNERS

Clint Murchison Jr. and Bedford Wynne were considered the co-owners of the Cowboys franchise when it was awarded, in 1960, but the reality is that Murchison owned 95 percent of the team. Murchison had inherited a fortune from his late father's oil business, and Wynne had his hand in a variety of businesses. What the men did best was decide to let general manager Tex Schramm, director of scouting and personnel Gil Brandt, and head coach Tom Landry run the football operation. Wynne sold his share of the Cowboys in 1967; Murchison kept control of the team until 1984, when he sold the franchise to H. R. "Bum" Bright.

5 TEX SCHRAMM

He was the original general manager of the Cowboys, but he was so much more. Schramm was one of pro football's great visionaries, helping to lead the NFL into its modern age. He's credited with a variety of innovations, among them installing a play clock, using instant replay, and moving the goalposts to the back of the end zone. It was Schramm who helped instigate the negotiations that led to the NFL-AFL merger. But it was the Cowboys where his brilliance and dedication were most evident, from the hiring of Tom Landry and Gil Brandt to the steady leadership that allowed the franchise to grow into more than just a football team.

Tom Landry and Tex Schramm at the 1960 NFL Draft

DALLAS COWBOYS

"*Tex will go down as one of the most influential figures in the history of the NFL.*"

—Don Shula

6 THE FIRST COWBOYS

The 1960 Cowboys were composed of 36 veterans plucked from the other 12 NFL teams. Each existing team could protect 25 players on its roster, and the Cowboys were allowed to pick three players from each team, forming the 36-player foundation for the new franchise. Needless to say, it wasn't a roster loaded with stars. Not surprisingly, the Cowboys struggled the first year, going 0–11–1. They managed a 31–31 tie at New York in their second-to-last game of the first season.

1960 game versus New York at Yankee Stadium

7 EDDIE LEBARON

LeBaron was the Cowboys' first star player, playing the last three seasons of his impressive career in Dallas with the new franchise. The Cowboys so coveted LeBaron that they traded their first pick in the 1961 NFL Draft (Dallas didn't have a pick in the 1960 draft) for the 5-foot-9 quarterback. He was the Cowboys' starting quarterback from 1960 through 1962, though he split time with Don Meredith. LeBaron, who was elusive and had a knack for leadership, was good enough in his final season that he made the Pro Bowl in 1962, despite having just a 4–21–1 record in three years as the Cowboys' quarterback. When LeBaron, who spent the bulk of his career with the Redskins, retired in 1963, he was the 11th-ranked passer in league history with 13,399 passing yards and 104 touchdown passes.

8 THE FIRST GAME

On September 24, 1960, the Cowboys hosted the Pittsburgh Steelers at the Cotton Bowl in the first regular season game in franchise history. There were two noteworthy numbers:

The Steelers won 35–28.

And the estimated attendance was 30,000, though that may have been higher than the true number of spectators who saw the first game.

9 THE STEERS

When Dallas was awarded an NFL franchise, it briefly used Steers as its nickname. Given the team's location in the heart of Texas, it made a lot of sense. However, the proposed moniker didn't last long. Team officials also considered calling the team the Rangers, another nickname with historical perspective, but when a local minor league baseball team also known as the Rangers decided not to fold in 1960, the NFL team settled on the Cowboys.

THe Cowboys' Tom Franckhauser (32) tries to break up a pass to Cleveland's Ray Renfro (26), 1960.

DeMarcus Ware (94) sacks Redskins quarterback Rex Grossman (8).

10 THE REDSKINS RIVALRY

The essence of sports competition can be defined by great rivalries. Yankees–Red Sox. Duke–North Carolina. Nicklaus-Palmer. In the NFL, it's the Cowboys and the Washington Redskins. In fact, it began before the Cowboys existed. Clint Murchison Jr., the Cowboys' original owner, tried to buy the Redskins from George Preston Marshall when he put them up for sale in the late 1950s. Close to making a deal, Marshall changed the terms and Murchison then decided to start a new expansion franchise in Dallas instead.

For more than 50 years, they've gone at each other with an uncommon fire. It was Don Meredith against Sonny Jurgensen. It was Tom Landry against George Allen. It was the Doomsday Defense against the Hogs. They've won eight Super Bowls between them and written a significant share of the league's history. Jimmy Johnson. Joe Gibbs. Emmitt Smith. Joe Theismann. Randy White. John Riggins. And on it goes.

11 COWBOY CHICKEN CLUB

Early in their rivalry, in 1961, some Cowboys fans decided to have fun at the expense of Redskins owner George Preston Marshall and spread chicken feed all over Washington's D.C. Stadium field to disrupt a Christmas halftime show that involved Alaskan sled dogs pulling Santa into the stadium. The plan was to release 76 chickens—which were hidden in the stadium—just before the dogs pulled Santa into the stadium. The idea was to sabotage the big show by having chickens clucking all over the field. It almost worked, but the chickens were discovered moments before they were to be released, and the stunt didn't come off.

A year later, after promising chickens in the stadium again, Cowboys fans unfurled four banners shortly before kickoff in D.C. that read CHICKENS. At the same time, two men in chicken outfits ran through the stadium tossing colored eggs to stunned fans. One man made it to the field, where he released a real chicken for another Cowboys victory over the Redskins.

Tom Landry talks with
Roger Staubach (12).

12 TOM LANDRY

To this day, no man may represent the Dallas Cowboys franchise better than Tom Landry, the team's first head coach. The record shows that Landry had a 270–178–6 record in his 29 seasons as the Cowboys' head coach, a career that included victories in Super Bowls VI and XII, five NFC championships, and 13 divisional titles.

But Landry can't be measured by numbers alone. His presence, cool and confident on the sideline wearing his ever-present fedora, came to personify the Cowboys. He was an innovator and a leader who arrived at the Dallas franchise after a stint as defensive coordinator of the New York Giants, where Vince Lombardi was the offensive coordinator. Landry was inducted into the Pro Football Hall of Fame in 1990, and his statue stands outside the new Cowboys Stadium.

13 THE LEADER

Tom Landry was a relatively quiet man, a devout Christian who believed deeply in certain principles that guided his life and his coaching. Among Landry's most memorable comments were these:

"I don't believe in team motivation. I believe in getting a team prepared so it knows it will have the necessary confidence when it steps on a field and be prepared to play a good game."

"Leadership is a matter of having people look at you and gain confidence, seeing how you react. If you're in control, they're in control."

"When you want to win a game, you have to teach. When you lose a game, you have to learn."

"Setting a goal is not the main thing. It is deciding how you will go about achieving it and staying with that plan."

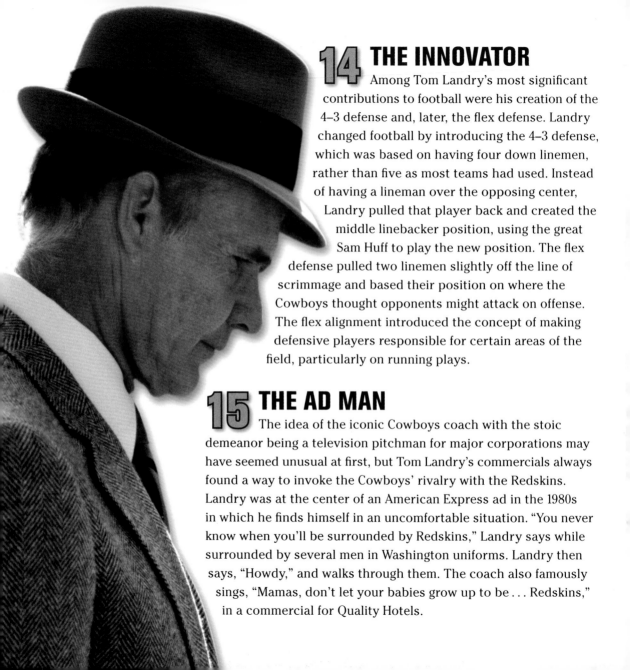

14 THE INNOVATOR

Among Tom Landry's most significant contributions to football were his creation of the 4–3 defense and, later, the flex defense. Landry changed football by introducing the 4–3 defense, which was based on having four down linemen, rather than five as most teams had used. Instead of having a lineman over the opposing center, Landry pulled that player back and created the middle linebacker position, using the great Sam Huff to play the new position. The flex defense pulled two linemen slightly off the line of scrimmage and based their position on where the Cowboys thought opponents might attack on offense. The flex alignment introduced the concept of making defensive players responsible for certain areas of the field, particularly on running plays.

15 THE AD MAN

The idea of the iconic Cowboys coach with the stoic demeanor being a television pitchman for major corporations may have seemed unusual at first, but Tom Landry's commercials always found a way to invoke the Cowboys' rivalry with the Redskins. Landry was at the center of an American Express ad in the 1980s in which he finds himself in an uncomfortable situation. "You never know when you'll be surrounded by Redskins," Landry says while surrounded by several men in Washington uniforms. Landry then says, "Howdy," and walks through them. The coach also famously sings, "Mamas, don't let your babies grow up to be . . . Redskins," in a commercial for Quality Hotels.

Tom Landry, left, and Tex Schramm break ground for the Cowboys' new facilities, 1983. Inset: Tom Landry

"The secret to winning is constant, consistent management."

—Tom Landry

16 THE FIRST WINNING SEASON

The Cowboys had their breakthrough year in 1966, their seventh season, when they went 10–3–1 and reached the NFC Championship Game, which they lost to Green Bay 34–27. A season after posting a 7–7 record, the Cowboys started fast, winning their first four games by an average score of 45–11. The Cowboys also closed fast, winning five of their last seven games as they elevated themselves to one of the league's new powers. Although the team had plenty of offensive stars, led by quarterback Don Meredith and wide receiver Bob Hayes, it was reinforced by a stout defense, which allowed just 254 yards per game. Bob Lilly, Chuck Howley, and Lee Roy Jordan anchored the squad that would define Dallas for years to come.

17 THOUSAND OAKS

For 27 summers, the Cowboys made their training camp home at California Lutheran College (later, University) in Thousand Oaks, just northeast of Los Angeles. It started in 1963 and became a part of the Cowboys' tradition, always heading west to get ready for the season. The CLU football practice field has since been replaced, and the building that housed the team has been transformed into family residences. In recent years, the Cowboys have trained in a variety of locations, including Oxnard, California, and Austin and San Antonio, Texas.

Chuck Howley (54) and Mel Renfro
(20) close in on Green Bay's Jim
Taylor (31), January 1, 1967.
Inset, left to right: Bob Lilly,
Chuck Howley, and Lee Roy Jordan

18 DON MEREDITH

On the list of most popular all-time Cowboys, Don Meredith ranks at or near the top of virtually everyone's list. Gil Brandt, the team's longtime director of scouting and personnel, called Meredith the original face of the franchise. Meredith and the Cowboys belonged together. He played high school football at Mount Vernon (Texas) High, played college ball at Southern Methodist University, and spent all nine of his NFL seasons in Dallas—a true Texan. After sharing time at quarterback with Eddie LeBaron early in his career, Meredith became the starter in 1963 and by 1966 was the NFL's player of the year. Known for his toughness and his personality, Meredith—who was originally drafted by the Chicago Bears before being traded to Dallas for a third-round draft choice—was an integral part in the evolution of the franchise. He finished his career with 17,199 passing yards and 135 touchdown passes.

19 DANDY DON

Don Meredith's fame increased after his retirement in 1968. Meredith became an actor, a commercial pitchman, and, most famously, a color commentator on ABC's groundbreaking *Monday Night Football*. Meredith's personality—he came across as a laid-back Texan who enjoyed life and liked to laugh—made him hugely popular.

Working in a booth with Howard Cosell and Frank Gifford, Meredith provided the perfect blend of levity and insight to one of the most famous broadcasting trios in sports history. Meredith's down-home style worked brilliantly against Cosell's nasal, condescending style that irritated millions of viewers. To this day, when a game gets out of hand near the end, commentators and fans will lapse into Meredith's famous "Turn out the lights, the party's over" refrain he introduced on *Monday Night Football*.

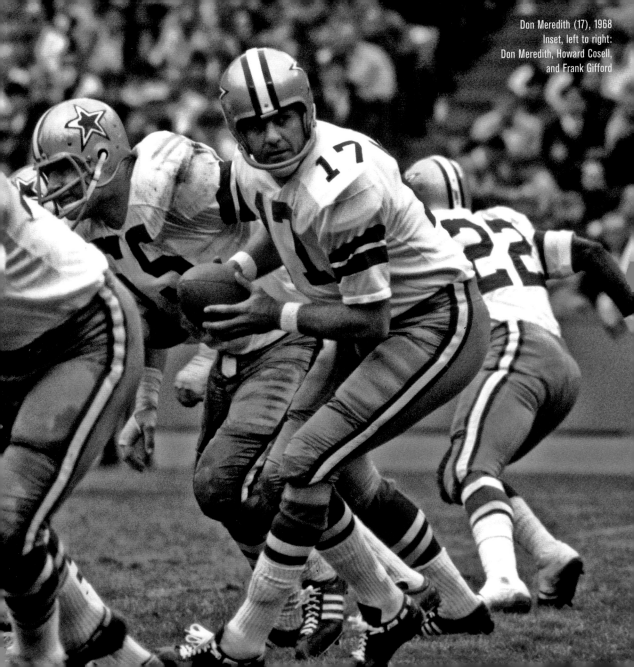

Don Meredith (17), 1968
Inset, left to right:
Don Meredith, Howard Cosell,
and Frank Gifford

Chuck Howley (54) returns an interception during Super Bowl VI.

20 CHUCK HOWLEY

His career was thought to be over after a 1959 knee injury in training camp with the Chicago Bears, but two years later, Howley returned to football and the Cowboys took a chance on him. He became one of their great linebackers, playing 13 seasons for Dallas. Howley had excellent speed despite the knee injury, and he became the first defensive player—and the first from a losing team—to be named MVP of the Super Bowl. Howley earned the distinction for his two interceptions and a fumble recovery in the Cowboys' 16–13 loss to Baltimore in Super Bowl V. Howley retired with 25 interceptions and 18 fumble recoveries.

21 THE COTTON BOWL

From 1960 until 1971, the Cotton Bowl was home to the Dallas Cowboys—one of the most famous football stadiums in the United States. The Cotton Bowl had been around for 31 seasons by the time the Cowboys began playing there. Located on the state fairgrounds, the Cotton Bowl hosted the 1966 NFL Championship Game, when Green Bay beat Dallas, 34–27. The Cowboys left after the 1970 season to play at their new Texas Stadium, but recent renovations have kept the Cotton Bowl relevant, especially in October when it hosts Texas and Oklahoma in the Red River Rivalry.

22 COWBELLES AND BEAUX

Before there were the Dallas Cowboys Cheerleaders, there was a group of guys and girls, mostly from area high schools, who served in a similar capacity. They were largely an afterthought, just a small piece of the Dallas football landscape in the 1960s. They didn't wear skimpy outfits or white boots. They didn't have their own calendars. And by 1970, they didn't have a chance against the new cheerleaders.

Don Perkins (43) runs through a gaping
hole versus the Redskins, 1967.

23 DON PERKINS

Perkins was one of the Cowboys' first truly special players, creating in his eight-year career a legacy that few would match. He was named the NFL's rookie of the year in 1961 and made the All-NFL team in 1962, a tribute to his relentlessness and his toughness as a running back. Perkins had a knack for eluding tacklers, and in his eight NFL seasons, he finished among the league's top 10 rushers each year. Perkins, who was preceded only by Bob Lilly in the Cowboys' Ring of Honor, had the first 100-yard rushing game in franchise history when he gained 108 yards against Minnesota in 1961.

Bob Hayes (22) returns a punt
versus Cleveland, 1967.

24 THE WORLD'S FASTEST MAN

Bob Hayes was considered the world's fastest man—based on his world-record times in the 60-, 100-, and 220-yard dashes as well as the 100-meter dash—and Bullet Bob became one of the Cowboys' all-time greats. His speed forced defenses to change the way they played the Cowboys. A great punt returner, Hayes excelled as a wide receiver, once catching nine passes for 246 yards against the Washington Redskins, in 1966—a team record until 2009. Hayes has the distinction of being the only man to have both a Super Bowl ring and an Olympic gold medal. He was inducted into the Pro Football Hall of Fame in 2009.

25 THE ICE BOWL

The 1967 NFL Championship Game remains among the most famous ever—and not just because it was played on a windy day at Green Bay's Lambeau Field, where the temperature was 15 degrees below zero. It was a rematch of the 1966 title game, won by Green Bay over Dallas, and it was another showdown between Tom Landry and Vince Lombardi. The conditions were so brutal that officials' whistles didn't work and multiple players would later be treated for frostbite.

The Cowboys had taken a 17–14 lead on a 50-yard halfback option pass from Dan Reeves to Lance Rentzel, but the Packers weren't finished. With 16 seconds remaining and no timeouts left, Green Bay quarterback Bart Starr followed Jerry Kramer's block into the end zone for a 1-yard touchdown that sent the Packers to their second straight Super Bowl.

"You can tell the real Cowboys. They're the ones with the frozen fingers and broken hearts."

—Tom Landry

Cowboys defensive end George Andrie (66) picks up a Bart Starr fumble as Jethro Pugh (75) looks on.

Atlanta's Tom Moore (21) is surrounded by Cowboys Bob Lilly (74), Chuck Howley (54), Mike Gaechter (27), and Jethro Pugh (75), 1967.

26 THE DOOMSDAY DEFENSE

The 1970s was a time of memorable football nicknames, particularly for defenses. Minnesota had its Purple People Eaters. The Rams had their Fearsome Foursome. Denver had the Orange Crush. But none was more ominous than the Cowboys' Doomsday Defense.

Jethro Pugh, Bob Lilly, George Andrie, Chuck Howley, Lee Roy Jordan, Dave Edwards, and D. D. Lewis. Cornell Green, Mel Renfro, Herb Adderley, and Cliff Harris. Randy White, Ed "Too Tall" Jones, Charlie Waters, Bob Breunig, and Benny Barnes. All of them—and more— were a part of the Cowboys' dreaded, dominating Doomsday Defense.

27 JETHRO PUGH

It seems pretty strange to think a 6-foot-6, 275-pound defensive tackle could be overlooked, but that's the way it was at times for Pugh. He was a rock along the Dallas defensive line for 14 seasons, from 1965 to 1978, leading the team in sacks five straight years, but he never made it to a Pro Bowl. Pugh, though, was a force—together with the great Bob Lilly, he helped anchor the Doomsday Defense that won five NFC titles in the 1970s.

Mel Renfro (20) deflects a pass to
Cleveland's Paul Warfield (42), 1968.
Inset: Lee Roy Jordan

28 LEE ROY JORDAN

In his 14 seasons with the Cowboys, from 1963 to 1976, Jordan was a ferocious force in the middle of the Dallas defense. A five-time Pro Bowl participant, Jordan was the Cowboys' all-time tackles leader (743) when he retired. Over the course of his stellar career, Jordan had 32 career interceptions and 18 fumble recoveries. In 1971, he had a team-record 21 tackles against Philadelphia. Jordan's finest moment may have come in the first quarter of a game against the Cincinnati Bengals, in 1973. In the space of five minutes, Jordan intercepted Bengals quarterback Ken Anderson three times, returning one of them for a 31-yard touchdown.

29 MEL RENFRO

For 14 seasons, from 1964 to 1977, Renfro anchored the Dallas secondary, moving from safety to cornerback in his fifth season, while building a Hall of Fame career. Renfro made the All-NFL first team five times and appeared in 10 Pro Bowls, largely for his play as a defensive back but also because he was one of the most dangerous special teams players in the league. He led the league with 10 interceptions in 1969 and finished his career with 52 interceptions, three of which he returned for touchdowns. Renfro's interception in the 1970 NFC Championship Game set up a winning touchdown drive that put the Cowboys in their first Super Bowl. He was inducted into the Pro Football Hall of Fame in 1996.

"He was a great competitor."

—Tom Landry, on Lee Roy Jordan

30 GIL BRANDT

While Tex Schramm ran the franchise and Tom Landry coached the team, Brandt brought together the pieces that made the Cowboys successful. For 29 seasons, from 1960 to 1988, he was in charge of the Cowboys' scouting and personnel decisions. The overarching success of the franchise speaks to Brandt's ability to evaluate talent. From Roger Staubach to Tony Dorsett to Emmitt Smith, from Blaine Nye to Harvey Martin to Tom Rafferty, Brandt was responsible for bringing them to Dallas, where success became perpetual.

31 DRAFTING ROGER STAUBACH

One of the sharpest moves the Cowboys pulled off came when they drafted Roger Staubach in the 10th round of the 1964 draft. It was surprising because Staubach still had one season of eligibility left at the Naval Academy, but since he had played one season at the New Mexico Military Institute, he was eligible for the draft. There was also the matter of Staubach's four-year commitment to serve in the Navy after his graduation from Annapolis. It didn't sway the Cowboys, who were content to wait for their next great quarterback.

32 MULTIPLE CHOICE

For parts of three seasons, Craig Morton and Roger Staubach shared the Cowboys' quarterback job—to the point that they actually alternated plays. Morton had been the team's first-round draft choice in 1965, and Staubach arrived four years later after a tour of duty in the Navy. Head coach Tom Landry tried to make the two-quarterback system work, but it became a consuming duel. Morton was a great downfield passer. Staubach was a supremely competitive leader. Both started Super Bowls for the Cowboys, but ultimately Morton was traded to the New York Giants. Later, Morton would land in Denver, where he and the Broncos squared off against Staubach and the Cowboys in Super Bowl XII.

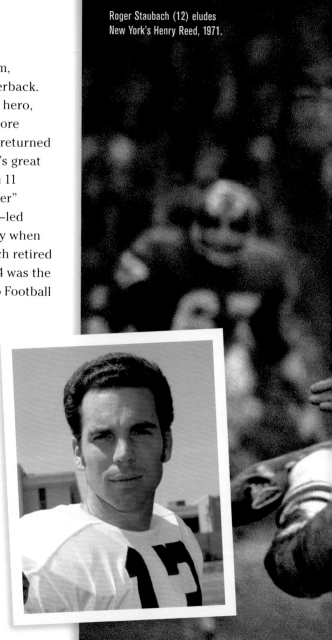

Roger Staubach (12) eludes New York's Henry Reed, 1971.

33 ROGER STAUBACH

If the Cowboys are America's Team, Staubach may have been Uncle Sam's quarterback. He was the quintessential American football hero, having won the Heisman Trophy at Navy before serving his country for four years. When he returned to football, Staubach became one of the NFL's great players, making six Pro Bowl appearances in 11 seasons. Staubach—whose "Roger the Dodger" nickname came from his scrambling ability—led the Cowboys to their first Super Bowl victory when he was MVP of Super Bowl VI. When Staubach retired from football, in 1980, his passer rating of 83.4 was the highest all-time. He was inducted into the Pro Football Hall of Fame in 1985.

34 ROGER THAT

When the *Dallas Morning News* polled its readers, in 2010, about their favorite Cowboys through the years, there was little doubt who the winner would be. It was Roger Staubach. It probably had to do with the fact that Staubach led the Cowboys on 23 game-winning drives in the fourth quarter, 17 of which came in the final two minutes or in overtime. These late-game heroics earned Staubach another nickname: "Captain Comeback."

"There are no traffic jams along the extra mile."

–Roger Staubach

Cowboys coach Tom Landry is carried from the field by his players, including Rayfield Wright (70), following Super Bowl VI.

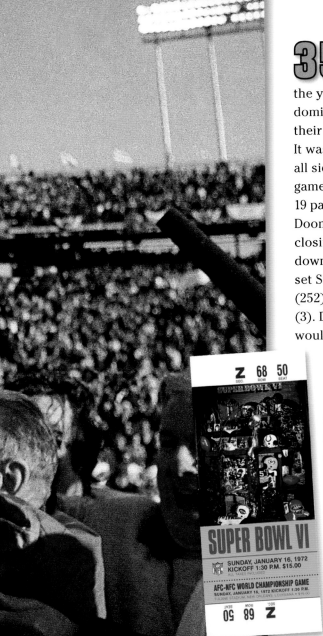

35 SUPER BOWL VI

After several near misses through the years, the Cowboys finally won the big one, dominating Miami 24–3 in New Orleans to claim their first Super Bowl victory, on January 16, 1972. It was a spectacular performance for Dallas on all sides. Quarterback Roger Staubach was the game's Most Valuable Player after completing 12 of 19 passes for 119 yards and two touchdowns. The Doomsday Defense throttled the Miami attack, closing the season by allowing just one touchdown over the final 29 quarters. The Cowboys set Super Bowl records for most rushing yards (252), first downs (23), and fewest points allowed (3). Dallas finally had a Super Bowl trophy. There would be more to come.

36 MIKE DITKA

He may be most closely linked to the Chicago Bears, but a significant portion of Ditka's career was tied to the Cowboys. He spent four seasons in Dallas as a tight end, playing from 1969 through 1972 and catching a touchdown pass in the team's Super Bowl VI win over Miami. After retiring, Ditka spent nine years on Tom Landry's staff as an assistant coach, setting up what would be an unforgettable run as the Bears' head coach starting in 1982.

37 BOB LILLY

When the Cowboys used their first-ever draft choice to pick defensive end Bob Lilly from Texas Christian University, it was one of the best investments in franchise history. Lilly came to be known as "Mr. Cowboy" for his relentless style, toughness, and personality. He played in a team-record 196 consecutive games and led the team in sacks in 1961, 1962, and 1963. A move to defensive tackle early in his career allowed Lilly to dominate the line to the point that he was named first-team All-NFL eight times, including six years in a row beginning in 1964. When Lilly was inducted into the Pro Football Hall of Fame in 1980, he became the first Cowboy enshrined.

38 THE 29-YARD SACK

It was late in the second quarter of the Super Bowl VI showdown between Dallas and Miami when Dolphins quarterback Bob Griese dropped back to pass. The Cowboys had a full rush on, and Bob Lilly, a great pass rusher, ripped through a hole in the Miami line and locked in on Griese. Seeing Lilly, Griese rolled to his right, only to find Cowboy Larry Cole coming at him from the other side. With no place to go but backward, Griese went into a full retreat, to no avail. Lilly finally ran him down, tackling him for a 29-yard loss that summed up the Cowboys' performance that day.

Left: Bob Lilly (74) chases down Miami's Bob Griese (12) in Super Bowl VI.

39 CALVIN HILL

Hill was the first Ivy League player—he graduated from Yale—to be a first-round NFL Draft choice, and he didn't disappoint. As a rookie, Hill took the league by storm until he suffered a broken toe late in the 1969 season. Still, Hill's impact was already being felt. After being slowed by injuries in 1970 and 1971, Hill became the first Cowboy to rush for 1,000 yards in a season when he gained 1,036 yards in 1972. He topped the 1,000-yard mark again the next season. Although he spent just six seasons in Dallas, Hill made the Pro Bowl four times and was an integral part of the Cowboys' first Super Bowl championship team in 1972.

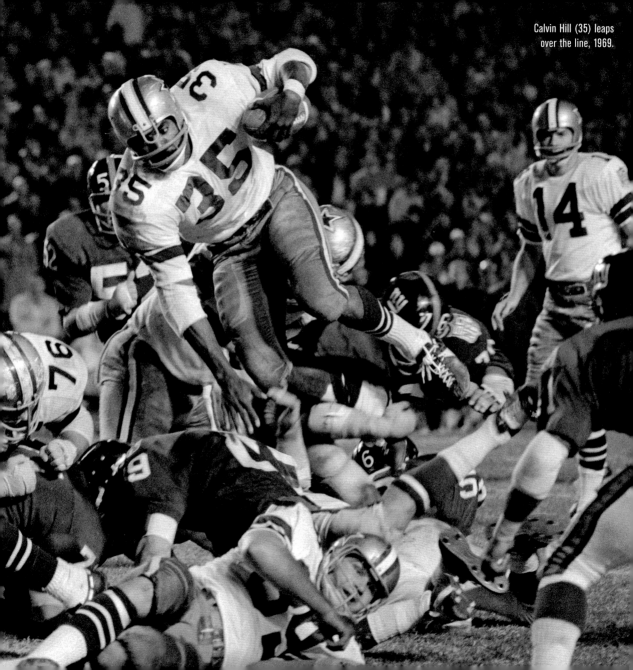

Calvin Hill (35) leaps
over the line, 1969.

Walt Garrison (32) tries to beat Pittsburgh's Joe Greene (75) to the corner, in 1972.

40 WALT GARRISON

Garrison was the Cowboys' true cowboy, a fullback who could both carry the ball up the middle and rope a steer if needed. For nine seasons, Garrison was an integral part of the Cowboys. He wasn't flashy but he was reliable, earning one Pro Bowl appearance in 1972. Garrison's fame remained after he retired when he became a well-known spokesman for Skoal smokeless tobacco, pitching the product with the line "Just a pinch between your cheek and gum..."

41 MONDAY NIGHT FOOTBALL

Since it began in 1970, *Monday Night Football* has been like a second television home to the Cowboys. They've been on *MNF* 72 times through 2011, second only to the Miami Dolphins. They've also been successful, posting a 43–29 record on Monday nights. However, it didn't start well for the Cowboys. In their first Monday night appearance, on November 16, 1970, the Cowboys lost 38–0 to the then–St. Louis Cardinals. Of the Cowboys' 72 Monday night appearances through 2011, 15 of them have come against the rival Washington Redskins.

"If it was third down and you needed four yards, if you'd get the ball to Walt Garrison, he'd get you five. And if it was third down and you needed 20 yards, if you'd get the ball to Walt Garrison, by God, he'd get you five."

—Don Meredith

Texas Stadium,
Thanksgiving Day,
1993

42 TEXAS STADIUM

On September 17, 1971, the Cowboys played the first game in their new stadium, a 65,675-seat facility in Irving, not far from the sprawling Dallas–Fort Worth airport. It became a part of the Cowboys, as much as the star on the helmet and the legacy of Tom Landry. Originally, team owner Clint Murchison Jr. proposed a stadium in downtown Dallas, but he couldn't make that happen, so the suburban site was selected instead. The Cowboys played their final game in Texas Stadium in 2008, losing to the Baltimore Ravens. Two years later, having been replaced by Cowboys Stadium, the original facility was demolished.

43 THE HOLE IN THE ROOF

The most recognizable feature of Texas Stadium was the hole in the roof, a design option that allowed fans to sit under cover while the game was played, in effect, outdoors. The original plan called for a retractable roof, but design issues prevented such a cover. It was linebacker D. D. Lewis who gets credited for saying the Texas Stadium roof was open "so God can watch his favorite team play."

"Wow, it's Texas Stadium. I was in awe."

—Emmitt Smith, recalling his first visit after being drafted by the Cowboys, in 1990

"I was always confident
I could perform in those
situations."

—Drew Pearson, on his late-game heroics

44 CLINT LONGLEY'S MOMENT

Longley was a rookie who'd never played in an NFL game when he got the call to go in on Thanksgiving Day in 1974, with the Cowboys trailing Washington 16–3 in the third quarter and Roger Staubach injured. What happened after was football magic. Longley threw two touchdown passes in less than nine minutes to put the Cowboys ahead, 17–16. When Washington regained the lead, Longley did it again, connecting with Drew Pearson on a 50-yard touchdown pass to win one of the most memorable games in Cowboys history. It was Longley's only moment with the team. He was released less than two years later after punching Staubach in training camp.

45 THE MIRACLE WORKER

When it came to big plays, few Cowboys have ever had a better flair for the dramatic than Drew Pearson. He caught Clint Longley's Thanksgiving Day prayer that beat the Redskins in 1974. He caught two touchdown passes in the final four minutes of a come-from-behind 1980 playoff win over the Atlanta Falcons. And, of course, he caught the famous Hail Mary pass against Minnesota, in 1975. Over the course of his 11-year career with the Cowboys, from 1973 to 1983, Pearson caught 489 passes for 7,822 yards—not bad for an undrafted free agent.

46 THE HAIL MARY PASS

The Cowboys were down to their last gasp, trailing Minnesota 14–10 with 24 seconds remaining in their 1975 divisional playoff game in Minneapolis. With the ball on the 50-yard line, quarterback Roger Staubach said "streak route" in the huddle and wide receiver Drew Pearson took off. As an orange thrown from the stands landed between Pearson and Vikings defensive back Nate Wright, Pearson pulled in the touchdown pass that stunned the Vikings crowd and a football nation.

Asked about the play afterward, Staubach said, "I closed my eyes and said a Hail Mary." The football dictionary had a new entry.

Drew Pearson (88) celebrates a touchdown reception versus Washington in the 1983 NFC Championship Game.

47 CLIFF HARRIS

For a safety who arrived in Dallas as an undrafted free agent from tiny Ouachita Baptist University, Harris went on to carve out a remarkable career in the Cowboys' secondary. In his 10-year career with the Cowboys, Harris intercepted 29 passes, but that's not the most impressive number in his Dallas résumé. Harris played in five Super Bowls, one of only 13 players to appear in the ultimate game that often. As part of a secondary that included Herb Adderley, Mel Renfro, Cornell Green, and Charlie Waters, Harris played his way to six Pro Bowls and a place in the Cowboys' Ring of Honor.

48 CHARLIE WATERS

Some guys just have a sense for how to play football, and Waters was a master at making the most of his talent. A former quarterback converted to defensive back, Waters played strong safety and teamed with Cliff Harris to form a dynamic duo at the back of the Dallas defense for many years. A three-time Pro Bowler, Waters played 12 seasons with the Cowboys, and the team made the playoffs 11 times. Waters was a ferocious hitter, but he also had a knack for making big plays. Of his 50 career interceptions, nine of them came in the playoffs, still a franchise record.

> *"Harris and Waters might as well have been actual brothers or even twins. They were so inseparable on and off the field that you almost thought of them as a single entity."*

—Roger Staubach, from *Tales from the Dallas Cowboys*

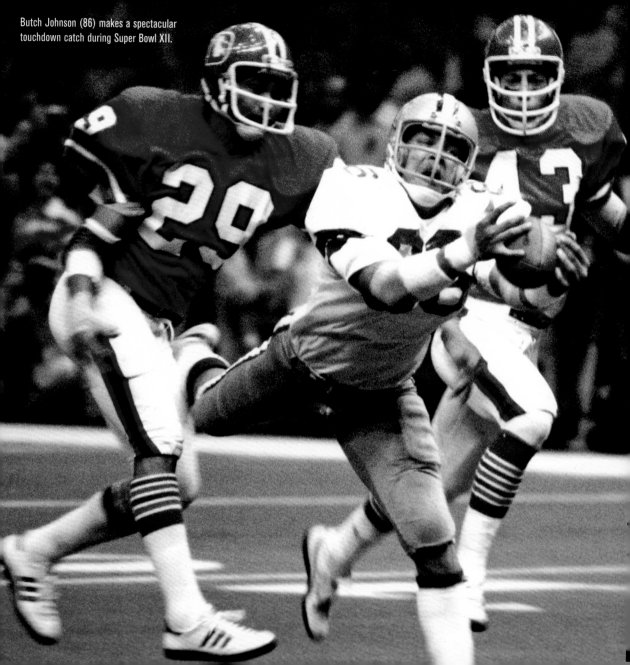

Butch Johnson (86) makes a spectacular touchdown catch during Super Bowl XII.

49 SUPER BOWL XII

The Cowboys won their second Super Bowl, defeating Denver 27–10 in New Orleans, in a game that focused on the duel between former teammates Roger Staubach and Craig Morton. It also matched Denver's famous "Orange Crush" defense led by Randy Gradishar and Tom Jackson against the "Doomsday Defense" led by Randy White and Ed "Too Tall" Jones. Virtually everything went the Cowboys' way as they overwhelmed the Broncos. The Cowboys' Butch Johnson made a spectacular fingertip catch for a touchdown on a pass from Staubach, and Dallas receiver Golden Richards hauled in a 29-yard halfback-option pass from Robert Newhouse for another touchdown. Meanwhile, Denver made seven first-half turnovers, and Morton, the league's comeback player of the year, never found an answer for the Dallas defense. White and fellow defensive lineman Harvey Martin were named co-MVPs for their part in what was a smothering defensive effort.

SUPER BOWL XII

AFC versus NFC for the NFL Championship and the Vince Lombardi Trophy
Sunday, January 15, 1978   5:00 P.M.   Louisiana Superdome, New Orleans

An Official Publication of the National Football League $2.50

"Roger told me to run a good post, and the rest is history."

—Butch Johnson, in *Sports Illustrated*

Jackie Smith (81) drops a potential touchdown pass in Super Bowl XIII.

"I never saw a more despondent player in the locker room than Jackie Smith after Super Bowl XIII."

–Tom Landry, on Jackie Smith

50 SUPER BLOOPER

Part of being a fan of any team means taking the tough moments with the thrilling ones. For Cowboys fans, there have been a few bitter moments that have lingered. It's part of the bargain fans make with their teams. One of those moments came in Super Bowl XIII when receiver Jackie Smith, good enough to earn a spot in the Pro Football Hall of Fame, dropped a wide-open 10-yard touchdown pass from Roger Staubach that would have tied the Cowboys with the Pittsburgh Steelers 21–21. Instead, the Cowboys, their fans, and Smith were left to wonder what might have been after a 35–31 loss to the Steelers.

51 THE UNIFORMS

Like a tuxedo on a man or a woman's little black dress, the Cowboys' uniforms are classics. They have remained essentially unchanged for the past 40 years, as instantly recognizable to football fans as the New York Yankees' pinstripes are to baseball fans. Metallic silver-blue pants with navy and white stripes down the outside of each leg and white jerseys with navy numbers and two matching stripes on the sleeves define the Cowboys, whose uniforms have often been voted the best in the league in a number of unofficial polls.

52 WHITE AT HOME

Prior to 1964, NFL rules required home teams to wear their darker jerseys. But when the rule was changed, the Cowboys chose to wear white at home. It became a tradition, a part of who the Cowboys are. In fact, the Cowboys have worn their white jerseys so often there have been suggestions that their rarely worn blue jerseys are bad luck. There's anecdotal evidence that suggests the Cowboys were snakebit for a time in their dark jerseys. That notion disappeared when the Cowboys debuted their version of an alternate jersey—blue with white shoulders and blue stars—a few years ago for special occasions.

Tony Romo (9) scrambles out of the pocket
in a 2011 game versus Washington.
Inset: Troy Aikman

53 TOO TALL JONES

At 6-foot-9, Ed Jones wasn't too tall. In fact, he was just right for 15 seasons with the Dallas Cowboys. Jones was the No. 1 overall pick in the 1974 NFL Draft, and his height made him a terror along the defensive line, using his wingspan to deflect passes or force quarterbacks to throw around him. Despite taking a season off to pursue a professional boxing career, in 1979—Jones went 6–0—"Too Tall" played in 224 games, the most by any Cowboy.

54 RANDY WHITE

They called him "the Manster" because he played as if he were half man, half monster. When the Cowboys made White the No. 2 pick in the 1975 NFL Draft, they put into motion a 14-year career for a linebacker turned defensive tackle who wound up in the Pro Football Hall of Fame, in 1994. White was a nine-time All-Pro player, earning NFC defensive player of the year honors in 1978. He finished his career with more than 1,000 tackles and 111 sacks. Perhaps most impressively, White missed just one game in his 14 seasons.

Randy White (54) sacks Philadelphia's
Ron Jaworski (7), 1983.

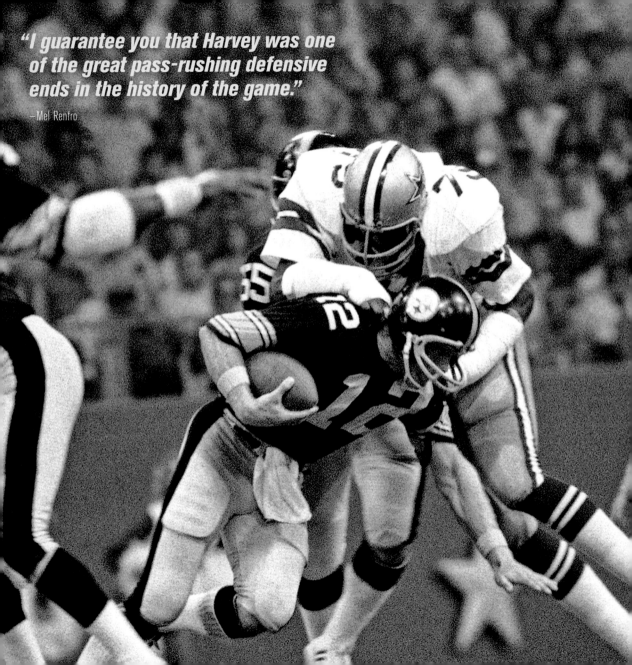

"I guarantee you that Harvey was one of the great pass-rushing defensive ends in the history of the game."

—Mel Renfro

55 HARVEY MARTIN

Playing on the opposite end from Ed "Too Tall" Jones, Martin established himself as one of the Cowboys' all-time greats while also becoming the first Dallas native drafted by his hometown team. Martin was named to the NFL's 1970s All-Decade Team and was a four-time Pro Bowler. Few players have ever had a better season than Martin had in 1977, when he was the league's defensive player of the year. In a 14-game season, Martin had 23 quarterback sacks among his 85 tackles as he set the standard for defensive end play.

56 HOLLYWOOD

There have been few players in Cowboys history who were more flamboyant than Thomas "Hollywood" Henderson. He spent five seasons with the Cowboys starting in 1975, using his speed and football sense to excel as a linebacker. But Henderson, who gave himself the "Hollywood" nickname, was his own worst enemy. His lifestyle and sideline antics eventually led the Cowboys to cut ties with him. Years later, Henderson emerged as a changed man, having kicked a serious drug habit, using his story to urge others to avoid the problems that nearly destroyed his life.

"I'm tall, talented, neat in the waist, cute in the face, and they call me 'Hollywood.' How can I lose?"

–Thomas "Hollywood" Henderson

65

57 THE DALLAS COWBOYS CHEERLEADERS

Only in Dallas could the cheerleaders be almost as famous as the team they support. When the Cowboys decided in 1972 to change the way they selected sideline cheerleaders, getting away from using local high schoolers, it began a dramatic transformation in the sport. The Cowboys went for sex appeal, and it worked. Wearing skimpy uniforms that included the Texas star and fringed vests—plus plenty of bare midriff—with go-go boots, and then, later, cowboy boots, the Cheerleaders changed forever the way sidelines looked at NFL games.

58 TRUE TEXAS STARS

The Cowboys Cheerleaders became so popular in the late 1970s that their celebrity reached far beyond football. In 1979, the Cheerleaders were the subject of a cheesy made-for-TV movie. The ratings were good enough that a sequel was done in 1980. They became guest stars on television shows, made USO tours in support of the military, and sold thousands of calendars each year. The Cowboys Cheerleaders have maintained their popularity over the decades, and the annual process of selecting members has been documented since 2006 in a reality series on Country Music Television.

59 DANNY WHITE

Patience paid off for Danny White. After a record-setting college career, White spent two seasons in the World Football League, then was Roger Staubach's backup for four seasons in Dallas before getting his chance as a starter, in 1980. White responded by throwing a franchise-record 29 touchdown passes that season, the first of three straight seasons in which he led the Cowboys to the NFC Championship Game. Also a punter, White passed for four or more touchdowns in a game eight times, and his 21,959 yards and 155 touchdown passes rank him among the most productive Cowboys of all time.

60 AN EVEN 20

From 1966 through 1985, Dallas never failed to have a winning season, an NFL record. Of those 20 seasons, the Cowboys won at least 10 games 16 different times.

"I would have to say the highlight of my career was just being a Dallas Cowboy."

—Danny White

61 TONY DORSETT

There haven't been many running backs as good and as graceful as Tony Dorsett, who spent 11 of his 12 exceptional seasons in the NFL playing for the Dallas Cowboys. A Heisman Trophy winner out of Pittsburgh, Dorsett had an immediate impact, rushing for 1,007 yards in his rookie season, in 1977. Dorsett didn't so much run as glide. He had speed, strength, and a gift for elusiveness. When he gained 1,646 rushing yards in 1981, Dorsett was one of the league's unstoppable forces. He accumulated 12,033 rushing yards for the Cowboys on his way to a spot in the Pro Football Hall of Fame.

62 99 YARDS

When the Cowboys broke huddle against Minnesota during a *Monday Night Football* game on January 3, 1983, Tony Dorsett was expecting teammate Ron Springs to take a handoff as the Cowboys tried to move the ball out from their own 1-yard line. Springs, though, had missed the call and had run off the field, thinking he wasn't supposed to be in on the play. The ball was snapped before anyone could call time-out, and Dorsett improvised. He slipped into a hole at the line of scrimmage, burst into daylight, and was gone. Dorsett's 99-yard run from scrimmage is the longest in NFL history—special enough that the shoes he wore are on display in the Pro Football Hall of Fame.

"To succeed, you need to find something to hold on to, something to motivate you, something to inspire you."

–Tony Dorsett

63 THE CATCH

It's one of the NFL's iconic moments, and it came at the Cowboys' expense. Dallas led the 1982 NFC Championship Game at Candlestick Park in San Francisco 27–21, but the 49ers had marched to the Dallas 11-yard line and faced third and three with 58 seconds remaining. The play was called "Red Right Tight— Sprint Right Option." Just before Ed "Too Tall" Jones knocked him to the ground, 49ers quarterback Joe Montana rolled right and floated a pass to Dwight Clark, who reached for the sky as Dallas defensive back Everson Walls looked on helplessly, unable to change history.

64 RAYFIELD WRIGHT

There haven't been many better offensive tackles in NFL history than Rayfield Wright, a seventh-round draft pick who wound up in the Pro Football Hall of Fame. He played 13 NFL seasons, all for the Cowboys, anchoring an offensive line that gave Roger Staubach time to throw and Tony Dorsett room to run. Once a tight end, Wright used his agility and toughness to dominate the right side of the Cowboys' offensive line.

65 BUM BRIGHT

After Clint Murchison Jr. and before Jerry Jones, there was Bum Bright. He bought the Cowboys—with multiple minority partners—from Murchison for $85 million, in 1984, but it was not the beginning of a golden age for the franchise. Dealing with his own financial problems and a team that was gradually going downhill in terms of its record, Bright finally sold the Cowboys to Jones for $140 million, in 1989, ending the shortest ownership era in the club's history.

Dwight Clark (87) makes the game-winning catch in the 1982 NFC Championship Game as Everson Walls (24) looks on.

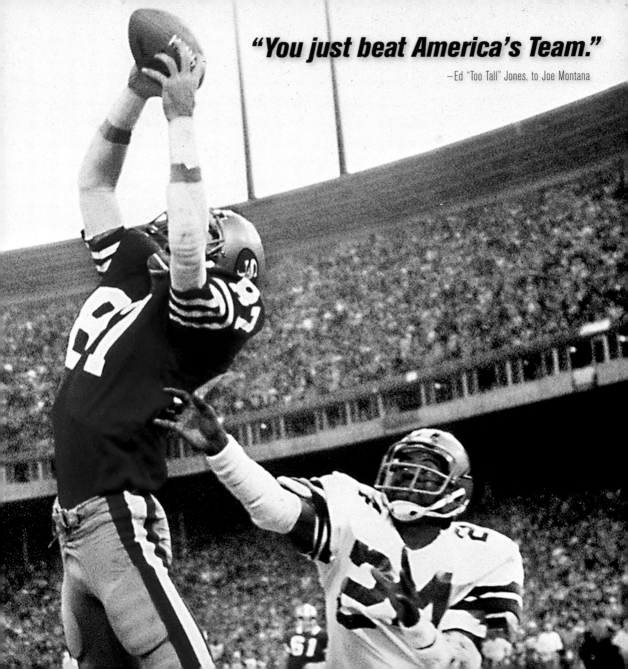

"You just beat America's Team."

—Ed "Too Tall" Jones, to Joe Montana

66 HERSCHEL WALKER

After playing three years in the short-lived United States Football League, Walker joined the Cowboys, who, suspecting he'd soon be out of a job when the USFL folded, had claimed him with a fifth-round pick in the 1985 NFL Draft. Walker was brilliant in Dallas. He played two years along Tony Dorsett, then took over as the team's primary offensive weapon in 1988, when he gained a combined 2,019 yards—only the 10th player in league history to accumulate 2,000 yards in a season. As good as he was, Walker lasted just two full seasons in Dallas before being traded to Minnesota, in 1989. Seven years later, Walker returned to the Cowboys and played his last two seasons in Dallas.

67 THE WALKER TRADE

In 1989, the Cowboys traded Herschel Walker to the Vikings—a trade that was unlike any other in NFL history. Walker was a huge star, but the Cowboys needed to start over. The Vikings, it turned out, needed a star. In a trade that's still talked about, the Cowboys sent Walker to Minnesota for five

players (linebackers Jesse Solomon and David Howard, running back Darrin Nelson, defensive back Issiac Holt, and defensive end Alex Stewart) and six draft choices. The Cowboys used those picks to add running back Emmitt Smith, defensive lineman Russell Maryland, and defensive back Darren Woodson to their roster, effectively changing the course of the franchise.

68 JERRY JONES

The Cowboys may be affectionately known as "America's Team," but in reality, they're Jerry Jones' team. He purchased the franchise from Bum Bright in 1989 for $140 million and immediately began a transformation that has kept the Cowboys among the most successful and recognizable sports franchises in the world. Jones has never been afraid to make a splash, and his firing of legendary coach Tom Landry upon taking ownership of the team sent an early message. Jones later admitted the matter could have been handled better, but it signaled his intention to be involved and to be aggressive. Although his hands-on style has bothered some, Jones has remained committed to making the Cowboys everything they can be.

69 WINNING JERRY'S WAY

When Jerry Jones took over the Dallas Cowboys in 1989, he wasted no time returning the franchise to glory. With aggressive moves that included the blockbuster trade of Herschel Walker to Minnesota and the hiring of Jimmy Johnson and, later, Barry Switzer as head coach, Jones rushed the Cowboys back into prominence. In his first seven years as the Cowboys' owner, Jones and the franchise picked up three Super Bowl victories, in 1992, 1993, and 1995. The team won six division titles in Jones' first 10 years as the owner. In the process, Jones added his name to a list that includes Art Rooney, Jack Kent Cooke, Al Davis, Eddie DeBartolo, and Robert Kraft as the only owners whose teams have won at least three Super Bowls.

Jerry Jones, right, greets Cowboys fans, 2011.

70 TROY AIKMAN

Like Roger Staubach before him, Aikman came to symbolize the Cowboys with his steady, remarkably successful on-field leadership. The No. 1 overall pick in the 1989 NFL Draft, Aikman went on to play 12 seasons with the Cowboys, leading them to three Super Bowl victories in the 1990s. Aikman wasn't flamboyant, leaving the flash to running back Emmitt Smith and wide receiver Michael Irvin, but he was consistently excellent. No quarterback won more games (90) in the decade of the 1990s than Aikman, who went 0–11 as a rookie, in 1989. The Cowboys' all-time passing leader, with 32,942 yards and 165 touchdowns, retired due to concussion issues in early 2001. Aikman was a shoo-in for the Pro Football Hall of Fame, in 2006, and went on to become one of the most respected football analysts on network television.

"Troy was all about the team. He was for winning… He could have passed for big yards if he wanted, but he did what was best for the team."

—Jerry Jones

71 JIMMY JOHNSON

There could hardly have been a more different successor to Tom Landry than Johnson, but he turned out to be exactly what the struggling franchise needed when he arrived. Brash, confident, and not afraid to mix it up with his owner and former Arkansas teammate Jerry Jones, Johnson put the fire back in the Cowboys. With shrewd drafting, aggressive coaching, and a relentless desire to succeed, Johnson masterminded the rebirth of the Cowboys' dynasty. In his first season in Dallas, Johnson—who guided the Miami Hurricanes to the 1987 college football national championship—posted a 1–15 record, but the times were changing. By 1992, Johnson and the Cowboys won Super Bowl XXVII. A year later, they repeated, winning Super Bowl XXVIII.

72 JIMMY AND JERRY

You might think that given their long relationship—Jerry Jones and Jimmy Johnson were college teammates at Arkansas—they were ideally suited to engineer the Cowboys' return to prominence. In one way they were. Together, they oversaw the team's dramatic turnaround from 1–15 to consecutive Super Bowl victories. However, the trophies didn't make everything beautiful. Jones and Johnson picked at each other publicly and privately even as the Cowboys were winning Super Bowls, and after five seasons together, they'd had enough of each other. Although their years together weren't always cordial and weren't always comfortable, Jerry Jones and Jimmy Johnson did find a way to win together.

Right: Jimmy Johnson
Inset: Jerry Jones, left,
and Jimmy Johnson

"Do you want to
be safe and good,
or do you want
to take a chance
and be great?"

– Jimmy Johnson

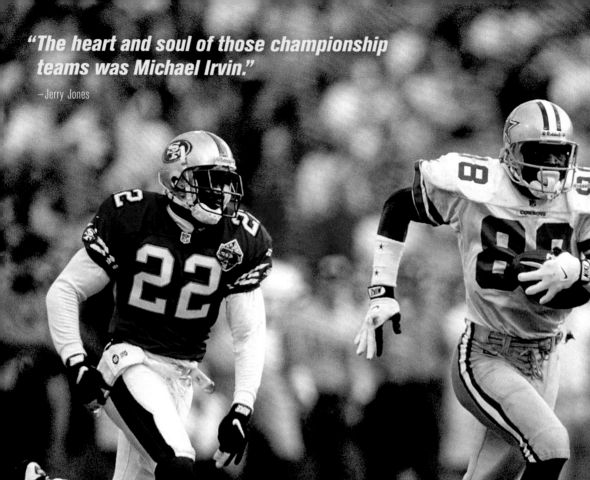

Michael Irvin (88) heads downfield after catching a pass in a game versus the San Francisco 49ers, 1995.

73 THE PLAYMAKER

The 15th of 17 children, Michael Irvin always had a flair for the dramatic. Whether it was the way he played, the way he carried himself, or the things he said, Irvin was impossible to ignore. When the Cowboys needed a game-changing wide receiver to go with quarterback Troy Aikman and running back Emmitt Smith, Michael Irvin was the perfect guy. With an ideal blend of size, speed, and swagger, Irvin gave the Cowboys the dangerous downfield threat they needed. Over the course of his 12-year career, from 1988 to 1999, Irvin caught 750 passes for 11,904 yards and 65 touchdowns. His 47 100-yard games are third most in NFL history. In Super Bowl XXVII, Irvin caught two touchdown passes in 18 seconds, a testament to his "Playmaker" nickname.

Michael Irvin

74 DARREN WOODSON

Other players got more attention during the Cowboys' three–Super Bowl run in the 1990s, but few were more valuable than safety Darren Woodson. From 1992 through 2004, Woodson was a fixture in the Dallas secondary, providing an enforcer-style toughness that helped define the defense. Woodson was good enough to make five Pro Bowl appearances, and he retired as the Cowboys' all-time leading tackler with 1,350 tackles.

75 BARRY SWITZER

In the larger-than-life world of the Dallas Cowboys, few have fit the personality model as well as Barry Switzer. When he succeeded Jimmy Johnson as the Cowboys' head coach, in 1994, Switzer brought the same swagger he had when he coached the Oklahoma Sooners, cementing their place among the top college programs. Switzer wasn't afraid to say what he felt, and he wasn't afraid to win big.

After guiding the Cowboys to a 12–4 record in his first season, Switzer took them all the way in 1995, leading them to a victory over Pittsburgh in Super Bowl XXX. To those who questioned whether Switzer's style would work in the NFL, the Lombardi Trophy answered the question. Like Johnson, Switzer is one of two coaches to win both the college football national championship and the Super Bowl.

Barry Switzer, 1994
Inset: Darren Woodson (28) tackles
New York's Tiki Barber (21), 2003.

Leon Lett (78) reaches for the loose ball after kicking it in the closing seconds of the Cowboys' Thanksgiving Day game versus the Dolphins, 1993.

76 SUPER BOWL XXVII

It had been 15 years since the Cowboys won a Super Bowl, and when they got the chance on January 31, 1993, they made the most of it. The Cowboys' 52–17 blowout of the Buffalo Bills was a case of football domination as the Bills lost their third straight Super Bowl. After spotting Buffalo a 7–0 first-quarter lead, the Cowboys took over—and took advantage of a record nine turnovers by the Bills. Quarterback Troy Aikman was his typically efficient self, completing 22 of 30 passes for 273 yards while earning Most Valuable Player honors. It was the first of two straight Super Bowl wins for the Jimmy Johnson–coached Cowboys and the start of a new era in the team's history. It's also worth remembering that the halftime entertainment at the Rose Bowl was provided by Michael Jackson.

77 LEON LETT

Lett spent 11 years in the NFL, 10 of them with the Cowboys, and he accumulated 22 career sacks, but he's best remembered for two boneheaded plays. The first came near the end of Super Bowl XXVII when Lett picked up a Buffalo fumble but, just before crossing the goal line, was stripped from behind by the Bills' Don Beebe, who knocked the ball out of the end zone for a touchback.

Then, on Thanksgiving Day 1993, the Cowboys were a play away from beating Miami in an icy, snowy game in Dallas. The Cowboys blocked the Dolphins' 41-yard field goal attempt, and the ball harmlessly skittered toward the end zone as several Dophins players surrounded it. With the game essentially over, if the ball was left untouched, Lett inexplicably slipped between a couple of Dolphins and inadvertently kicked the ball. Miami recovered the suddenly live ball at the 1-yard line and then kicked the game-winning field goal as time expired.

78 EMMITT SMITH

It's easy to judge Emmitt Smith's impact by the numbers, and the collection is spectacular. But Smith, who played for the Cowboys from 1990 through 2002, was more than one of the best running backs ever to play. Along with quarterback Troy Aikman and receiver Michael Irvin, Smith was part of the Cowboys' famous "Triplets," who defined one of the most successful runs any franchise has ever had.

Smith had an almost elegant running style. He had power, but wasn't a bulldozer. He had speed, but wasn't a sprinter. What he had was a combination of skills that made him durable, reliable, and the most productive running back in NFL history. And a first-ballot Hall of Famer.

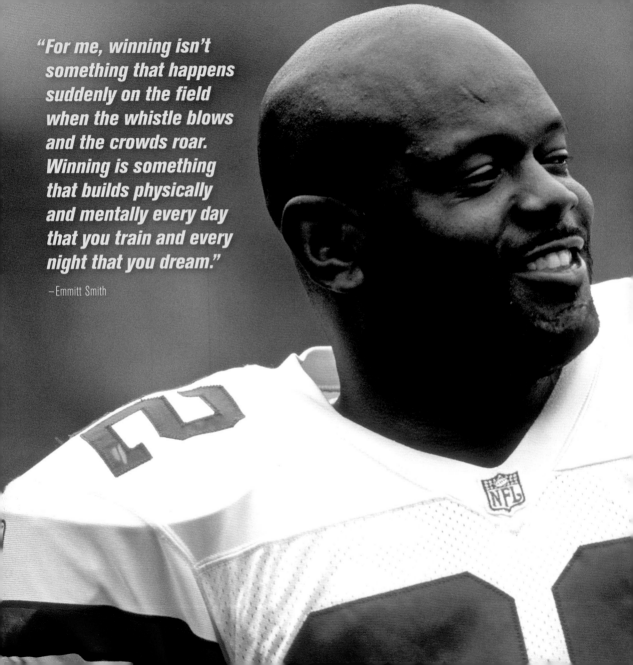

"For me, winning isn't something that happens suddenly on the field when the whistle blows and the crowds roar. Winning is something that builds physically and mentally every day that you train and every night that you dream."

—Emmitt Smith

79 EMMITT'S BEST

Smith's greatest season, 1993, didn't begin well—he missed the first two games due to a contract dispute. But once Smith started playing, he was practically unstoppable. Smith led the league with 1,486 rushing yards, earning himself the NFL MVP award. In the regular season finale against the New York Giants, Smith played through a separated shoulder as the Cowboys locked down home field advantage in the playoffs. Smith was exceptional through the playoff run, winning MVP honors in Super Bowl XXVIII and becoming the only player to win both MVP awards and the rushing title in the same season.

80 THE EMMITT SMITH COLLECTION

Here's a glimpse at the remarkable records set by Smith, who retired as the NFL's all-time leading rusher:

– Career rushing yards: 18,355 (1st all-time)

– Rushing touchdowns: 164 (1st all-time)

– Total touchdowns: 175 (2nd all-time)

– One of four runners to lead the NFL in rushing three or more seasons in a row, joining Steve Van Buren, Jim Brown, and Earl Campbell

– Consecutive 1,000-yard rushing seasons: 11

– Postseason rushing yards: 1,586 (1st all-time)

James Washington (37) returns a Buffalo fumble for a touchdown in Super Bowl XXVIII.

81 SUPER BOWL XXVIII

Super Bowl XXVIII once again pitted the Cowboys versus the Buffalo Bills—the first time in Super Bowl history that the same teams met in consecutive years. As before, the Cowboys prevailed again, beating Buffalo 30–13. The Cowboys found themselves trailing 13–6 at halftime, raising the possibility that the Bills—after three straight losses in the Super Bowl—might finally get a victory. It wouldn't happen. Behind Emmitt Smith's 132 rushing yards and a spectacular game by free safety James Washington, who had a fumble recovery for a touchdown and an interception, the Cowboys outscored the Bills 24–0 in the second half as they rolled to a second straight Super Bowl victory.

"I was never good.
I was always great."
—Deion Sanders

82 DEION SANDERS

For five seasons, "Prime Time" called Dallas home, and in those five seasons, Deion Sanders showed why he's considered one of the finest athletes in NFL history. The Cowboys won a free-agent sweepstakes to land Sanders, whose coverage skills at cornerback practically forced teams to throw away from him. But Sanders, who played for the Cowboys from 1995 through 1999, was more than a defensive back. He was an exceptional return man and could play receiver if needed. Sanders wasn't afraid of the spotlight, practically bringing it with him when he arrived in Dallas, but he proved to be every bit as good as advertised, making four Pro Bowl appearances in his limited time with the Cowboys.

83 DOUBLE RETURNS

Leave it to Deion Sanders to take full advantage of the big stage. Playing a Monday night game against the New York Giants in 1998, Sanders was at his high-stepping best. He broke open a scoreless game in the second quarter when he returned a punt 59 yards to give the Cowboys a 7–0 lead. He was just getting started. In the fourth quarter, Sanders capped the Cowboys' 31–7 victory over their rivals by intercepting a pass and taking it 71 yards for his second touchdown of the game.

84 NATE NEWTON

Big Nate was one of the all-time great offensive linemen for the Cowboys, with a style and personality as big as Newton himself. After being cut by the Washington Redskins and playing two seasons in the USFL, Newton landed in Dallas and became part of a tremendous offensive line that included Mark Tuinei, Mark Stepnoski, Erik Williams, and Larry Allen. Newton, who approached 400 pounds at one time, had a legendary appetite, even posing for photographs with the mounds of food he could consume. He made it work, though, earning six Pro Bowl appearances in his 13 seasons with the Cowboys.

85 LARRY ALLEN

How do you define greatness in an offensive lineman? Take a look at Allen's career. He played 14 NFL seasons (12 with the Cowboys), and he made the Pro Bowl in 11 of those seasons. Seven times, Allen was named All-Pro. When the NFL's All-Decade Team for the 1990s was announced, Allen was on it. Through his career, Allen played both offensive guard and tackle spots, helping buy time in the pocket for quarterback Troy Aikman and clearing holes for running back Emmitt Smith. And, by the way, he once bench-pressed 700 pounds.

Nate Newton

Larry Allen

86 THE FANS

The Cowboys may be based near Dallas, but they belong to the world. Their fans are scattered not just across Texas but across the country and around the world. There are fan clubs and chat rooms and Facebook pages connecting a legion of lovers tied to America's Team. Walk into a sporting goods store in Nebraska or North Dakota, New York or North Carolina, and you'll find something bearing the Cowboys' familiar star. Cowboys merchandise annually ranks at or near the top of league sales. And if you really want to know how deep the passion for the Cowboys runs, just check out the crowd when Dallas is on the road. Cowboys fans won't be hard to find.

87 CRAZY RAY

Wilford Jones, also known as "Crazy Ray" and "Whistling Ray," was such a fan of the Dallas Cowboys that he has a small place in the Pro Football Hall of Fame section dedicated to passionate fans. With his western-style outfits, his magic tricks, his shrill whistle, and his outsize personality, Jones was a part of the Cowboys' game day experience for most of their existence. He began selling pennants at games in 1962 and would miss only three home games in 46 years before passing away in 2007.

Cowboys fan

Crazy Ray

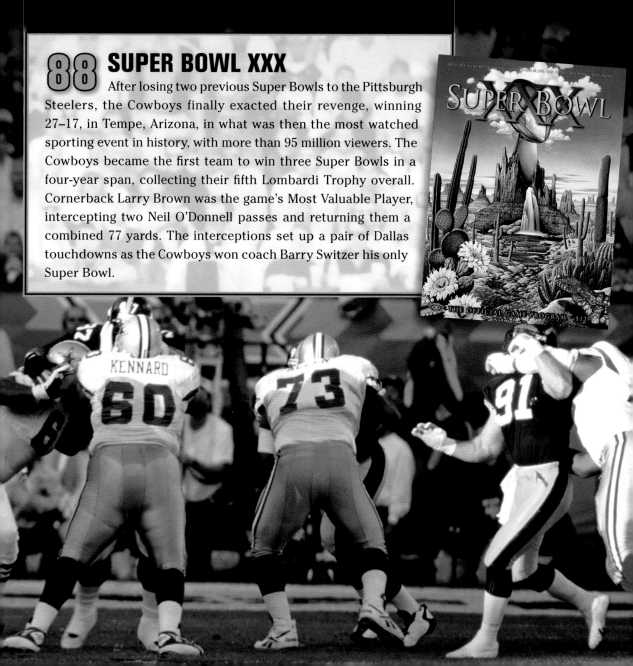

88 SUPER BOWL XXX

After losing two previous Super Bowls to the Pittsburgh Steelers, the Cowboys finally exacted their revenge, winning 27–17, in Tempe, Arizona, in what was then the most watched sporting event in history, with more than 95 million viewers. The Cowboys became the first team to win three Super Bowls in a four-year span, collecting their fifth Lombardi Trophy overall. Cornerback Larry Brown was the game's Most Valuable Player, intercepting two Neil O'Donnell passes and returning them a combined 77 yards. The interceptions set up a pair of Dallas touchdowns as the Cowboys won coach Barry Switzer his only Super Bowl.

"*There is winning and there is misery.*"

–Bill Parcells

89 BILL PARCELLS

Widely regarded as one of the game's great coaches, Parcells was hired by Jerry Jones to lead the Cowboys in 2003 after three straight 5–11 seasons. Parcells, with his no-nonsense style, immediately led Dallas to the playoffs with a 10–6 record in his first season. But that would be as good as it would get in Parcells' four years as the Cowboys' head coach. It was an unsettled time for the team, especially at quarterback, where Quincy Carter, Vinny Testaverde, and Drew Bledsoe had limited success. In 2006, his final season as head coach, Parcells replaced Bledsoe with Tony Romo, launching a new era in the team's history. Parcells finished with a 34–32 record as the Cowboys' head coach.

90 MOOSE

Fullback Daryl Johnston is living proof that a player's contribution can't be judged solely on statistics. Few Cowboys have been more popular than Johnston, who picked up his nickname, "Moose," from quarterback Babe Laufenberg. Johnston was brilliant in his 11-year career, whether catching passes, running up the middle, playing special teams, or blocking for Emmitt Smith. Johnston was a member of three Super Bowl–winning teams and went on to become a top NFL analyst. When Smith became the NFL's all-time rushing leader, he told Johnston, "I couldn't have done it without you."

"It was my pleasure. I couldn't imagine doing it for anybody else," Johnston replied.

Daryl Johnston (48) blocks for Emmitt Smith (22).

91 TONY ROMO

Undrafted out of college, Romo signed with the Cowboys as a free agent, in 2003, and stayed in the background until the 2006 season, when he became the new face of the franchise. When coach Bill Parcells named Romo the starting quarterback for a Sunday night game against the Carolina Panthers, it was a pivotal moment for Romo and the Cowboys. He led the team to the playoffs in 2006, and became a huge star because of it. Romo has had great highs, and crushing lows, the worst of which may be a botched hold on a potential game-winning field goal that cost the Cowboys a playoff game in Seattle.

"I play the game with passion. I enjoy the game. It's a lot of fun when I'm out there."

—Tony Romo

Jason Witten (82)
hauls in a pass as
two Lions defenders
converge, 2011.

92 JASON WITTEN

Witten is one of those special players who have helped define the position they play. As a tight end, Witten developed into one of the Cowboys' most dangerous and reliable offensive weapons. An excellent blocker and a superb receiver, Witten became Tony Romo's go-to receiver. That was never more true than in a December 2007 game against Detroit, when Witten tied an NFL record for tight ends by catching 15 passes. He will likely end up second on the all-time receptions list for tight ends. At 6-foot-6, 265 pounds, Witten used his size to become a hard-to-miss target for Romo and a harder-to-stop receiver for opponents.

93 TO'S BIG DAY

Cowboys receiver Terrell Owens had one of his greatest days on November 18, 2007—on the same field where he once infamously stomped on the Dallas star at midfield as a member of the San Francisco 49ers. In the 28–23 victory over the rival Washington Redskins, Owens scored all four Dallas touchdowns, catching passes from quarterback Tony Romo. Each scoring pass got progressively longer and more dramatic. The first was 4 yards, followed by a 31-yarder and a 46-yarder. Then, midway through the final quarter, Owens caught a 52-yard TD pass to help secure the victory. Although Owens had some turbulent moments in his three full seasons in Dallas, he twice led the league in touchdown receptions.

Terrell Owens

94 COWBOYS STADIUM

Simply put, there's nothing quite like it. At a cost of more than $1 billion, Cowboys Stadium is the largest domed stadium in the world and a fitting home to a franchise that is more than a football team. It has a retractable roof with a membrane-covered hole in the middle, reminiscent of the famous hole in the top of Texas Stadium. It seats 80,000 fans, though as many as 110,000 can squeeze in to see football. Special touches, including standing room concourses, restaurants, and the Cowboys' entrance to the field through a gathering place for fans, have made Cowboys Stadium an architectural marvel.

The big screen in Cowboys Stadium

95 THE BIG SCREEN

Living up to the "everything's bigger in Texas" concept, the 72-by-160-foot video board in Cowboys Stadium is a large part of the experience in attending an event at "Jerry's World." To call it a video board doesn't do it justice. Designed by Mitsubishi at a cost of $40 million, the board stretches from one 20-yard line to the other. On each end, there are 48-foot-wide screens for fans seated in the end zones. With 30 million lightbulbs and a total weight of more than one million pounds, the video board was the largest in the world when the stadium opened in 2009. On game days, eight cameras are used to beam images to the big board.

96 THE RING OF HONOR

For the greatest Cowboys, one of the highest honors is being inducted into the Ring of Honor inside the stadium. It was the idea of former president/general manager Tex Schramm, who would later be the 12th man inducted into the Ring. He began the tradition in 1975 by honoring defensive tackle Bob Lilly, who had recently retired. Lilly returned in uniform for his induction, and so began a touching piece of the Cowboys' story. There are 20 names in the Ring of Honor. They are Bob Lilly, Don Meredith, Don Perkins, Chuck Howley, Mel Renfro, Roger Staubach, Lee Roy Jordan, Tom Landry, Tony Dorsett, Randy White, Bob Hayes, Tex Schramm, Cliff Harris, Rayfield Wright, Troy Aikman, Michael Irvin, Emmitt Smith, Drew Pearson, Charles Haley, and Larry Allen.

97 DEMARCUS WARE

When the Cowboys used the 11th pick in the 2005 draft on Ware, an outside linebacker from Troy University, they landed one of the most productive pass rushers the game has seen. An ideal blend of speed, strength, and tenacity, Ware became the rare defensive player who often forced opponents to account for him with more than one blocker. Ware's relentlessness is evident on the field and on the stat sheet. In 2008, Ware had a quarterback sack in 10 straight games, tying an NFL record. He went on to have 20 sacks in the season. After having eight sacks as a rookie in 2005, Ware recorded double-digit sacks in each of the next six seasons, establishing himself as a rare force.

98 DEMARCO MURRAY'S DAY

Murray was listed as the Cowboys' second-team running back prior to the Week 7 game against the St. Louis Rams in 2011, but everything changed in one afternoon for the rookie third-round draft choice from Oklahoma. Murray was virtually unstoppable, rushing for a franchise-record 253 yards on 25 carries as he exploded onto the national scene. Murray's 253 yards shattered the Cowboys' single-game rushing record of 237 yards, set by Emmitt Smith in 1993. Murray's total was the 10th highest in NFL history. The day was highlighted by a 91-yard touchdown run, second only to Tony Dorsett's famous 99-yard sprint, in 1983.

DeMarco Murray (29) versus the Rams, 2011

DeMarcus Ware rushes the quarterback, 2011.

Roger Staubach (12) consults
with coach Tom Landry, 1972.

99 HALL OF FAMERS

If you visit Canton, Ohio, to immerse yourself in the history of professional football, you'll notice a large contingent of Cowboys among the honorees. Nineteen players and administrators with ties to the Cowboys are enshrined at Canton. Although a handful played the bulk of their careers elsewhere, each had an impact on the franchise. The honorees are Herb Adderley, Troy Aikman, Lance Alworth, Mike Ditka, Tony Dorsett, Forrest Gregg, Bob Hayes, Michael Irvin, Tom Landry, Bob Lilly, Tommy McDonald, Mel Renfro, Deion Sanders, Tex Schramm, Emmitt Smith, Jackie Smith, Roger Staubach, Randy White, and Rayfield Wright.

100 CONFERENCE CHAMPIONSHIPS

There have been 10 of them, dating back to the days before the NFL-AFL merger. Dallas won the NFL Eastern Conference title in 1966 and 1967. The Cowboys' league-leading eight NFC championships were won in 1970, 1971, 1975, 1977, 1978, 1992, 1993, and 1995.

101 THE SUPER BOWLS

Eight times, the Cowboys have made it to the NFL's biggest game, a number matched only by the Pittsburgh Steelers. Five times—1971 (VI), 1977 (XII), 1992 (XXVII), 1993 (XXVIII), and 1995 (XXX)—the Cowboys have won the Super Bowl, the second most in history.

Tom Landry is carried off the field following the Cowboys' 24–3 victory over Miami in Super Bowl VI.

1971

1977

1992

1993

1995

Tony Romo (9) throws a pass versus the Rams, 2011.

ACKNOWLEDGMENTS

If there are at least 101 reasons to love the Dallas Cowboys, there are many other reasons to love a project like this one.

It's a collaborative effort, with the work of many coming together to produce a book such as this one and others we've done in the series.

Thanks go to Mary Tiegreen, who had the vision and spirit to bring this series of books to life, touching on the simple but real people and events that fuel the unending passion of sports fans.

Writers know the value of good editors, and thanks go to Jennifer Levesque and her team at STC that includes managing editor Jen Graham, copy editor Richard Slovak, production manager Tina Cameron, and assistant editor Wesley Royce. They provide a comfort level that is invaluable.

Thanks to my brother, Dave, who uses his imagination and creativity to bring these books to life. It's a rare privilege to be given a chance to work with a member of your family.

Thanks also to those who helped with the photos, Yvette Reyes and her associates at AP Images, as well as Kevin Kelly at Getty Images.

To the Dallas Cowboys and their legion of fans, thanks for the moments, the memories, and the meaning of Cowboys' football, which belongs not just to Dallas but to our football-crazed nation.

And thank you to my family for your love and support in all things.

A Tiegreen Book

Published in 2012 by Stewart, Tabori & Chang
An imprint of ABRAMS

Library of Congress Cataloging-in-Publication Data

Green, Ron, 1956–
  101 reasons to love the Cowboys / by Ron Green.
     p. cm.
  ISBN 978-1-58479-982-5
1. Dallas Cowboys (Football team)—Miscellanea. 2. Dallas Cowboys (Football team) —History. I. Title. II. Title:
One hundred one reasons to love the Cowboys. III. Title:
One hundred and one reasons to love the Cowboys.
  GV956.D3G75 2012
  796.332'6407642812–dc23
                              2012003809

Text copyright © 2012 Ron Green Jr.
Compilation copyright © 2012 Mary Tiegreen

Editor: Jennifer Levesque
Designer: David Green, Brightgreen Design
Production Manager: Tina Cameron

101 Reasons to Love the Cowboys is a book
in the 101 REASONS TO LOVE™ series.

101 REASONS TO LOVE™ is a trademark
of Mary Tiegreen and Hubert Pedroli.

Printed and bound in China

10 9 8 7 6 5 4 3 2 1

Stewart, Tabori & Chang books are available at special
discounts when purchased in quantity for premiums
and promotions as well as fundraising or educational
use. Special editions can also be created to specification.
For details, contact specialsales@abramsbooks.com or
the address below.

THE ART OF BOOKS SINCE 1949

115 West 18th Street
New York, NY 10011
www.abramsbooks.com

PHOTO CREDITS

All photos are courtesy of AP Images, except for
"the Catch" on pages 72–73, which is courtesy of
Getty Images.

Super Bowl XXX ring